This page is intentionally left blank.

© 2023 Akeelah Publishing House.

Trisheena Bolakale

Pieces of the Pieces: A Literary Compilation of Love, Pain, Trauma and Growth.

All rights reserved. No part of this publication may be reproduced, stored in a retrieval system or transmitted in any form or by any means, electronic, mechanical, photocopying, recording or otherwise without the prior permission of the publisher or in accordance with the provisions of the Copyright, Designs and Patents Act 1988 or under the terms of any licence permitting limited copying issued by the Copyright Licensing Agency.

Published by: Akeelah Publishing House

Text Design by: Trisheena Bolakale

Cover Design by: Trisheena Bolakale

A CIP record for this book is available from the Library of Congress Cataloging-in-Publication Data

ISBN-13: 979-8-9876772-0-9

Pieces of the Pieces
A LITERARY COMPILATION OF LOVE, PAIN, TRAUMA AND GROWTH.

Akeelah Publishing House

TRISHEENA BOLAKALE

This book is dedicated to all of the people who have represented Purple Flowers in my life and throughout my life.
Thank you.
It was your love, grace and support that has kept me present. There are far more than are mentioned here. I am eternally grateful to you.

Trisheena Bolakale

PIECES OF THE PIECES
A LITERARY COMPILATION OF LOVE, PAIN, TRAUMA AND GROWTH
Akeelah Publishing House

Contents

7 Trigger Warning

8 Introduction

10 Dear Casey, Love Trisheena

(Trigger Warning: Abuse, Child Endangerment)

11 *Self*

12 Fulfilled

13 mybodyisatemple

(Trigger Warning: Sexual Abuse, Child Abuse, Rape)

16 I'm am here

18 Self Validation

19 It Was Angels Who Guided Me Home

21 Those Eyes

(Trigger Warning: Child Endangerment)

22 Just Breath

24 Purple Flowers

(Trigger Warning: Child Endangerment and neglect)

31 *Love*

32 Serving You MY Flowers

33 I've Let Them Go Ya'll

(Trigger Warning: PTSD & Anxiety Symptoms)

36 Deep Breath

37 Don't Get Too Used To Just Enough

39 Light Incoming

41 *Journey*

Trigger Warning

This book is a journey through some traumatizing experiences in my lifetime. This book is not about me losing my power. This book explores my actualization of it. I have found myself in the despair of depression in the past, not really knowing why I felt so heavy all of the time. I never took the time to hear myself. I had to hear myself cry out about the things that have hurt me. That have stunted my growth. I had to learn to call my trauma by name! And then pour so much love there. I have, within the balance of trauma love, pain and growth, decided to be the woman that I choose to be and live the life that best suits me. It's okay to put this trauma down. I tell my story for the little girl who got in the back of a van outside of my summer camp, whom I never saw a missing persons report for. I tell my story for the adults who bear the heaviness of codependency from the muck of toxicity.

Please take heed of the trigger warnings. Descriptive language is used. Protect yourself. Put yourself in a place where you don't have to absorb my heaviness. These stories are true to the best of my memory. Painful memories. These stories have caused me to cry out in agony, but ultimately made me treat myself with love and tenderness, and compassion. These stories are not about anyone who has violated me, I have made peace with their wrongdoings and wish them the karma that they deserve. This story is about me. My trauma, my pain, my love and my growth. And lots of people out there who need help with finding their voices.

Introduction

Hello! My name is Trisheena. A name that my father thought of when he combined Katrina and Patricia. Funny enough I was always called Casey instead though. I have reached a level of peace in my life that is still rough around the edges. Yes!! My peace is rough around the edges. Let me tell you why! I was in a therapy session and my therapist looked me in my face via zoom (well... pandemic) and asked me why I continue to let people mistreat me. She really had the NERVE to ask me that. I said what? The look of puzzled snatched my face. I'm not mistreated...

She said "Every one of the people that you have described to me has mistreated you. And I'm not largely concerned about them. People will do what we allow. I'm concerned about you. Why do you allow it?"

I go through things, but I'm not mistreated. At first, I said it with certainty. I asked myself that question maybe a thousand times before the tears started. This unmitigated launch into self-discovery was rough, but I looked at myself in the mirror and I promised myself that I would begin to choose me. Whatever happened in the past is done, I made peace with it. It made me reflect and ask not only what I wanted out of life ... but it made me question everyone and everything. Why this and why that. I have a crazy detailed memory and so many memories came flooding into my head. It was like childhood trauma really wanted to square up. I had to learn to not only understand Codependency, trauma, depression and anxiety. I had to learn to love on those broken pieces and make space for them. I had to learn to put them down when it was time. I had to learn to love me depressed or happy, productive or in bed. I had to rediscover myself, make peace with a very broken little girl and prepare myself to walk in the light that has beautifully guided me.

Welcome to my journey through love, pain, trauma and growth, but please don't forget to see the Purple Flowers.

Dear Casey, How is your day going young lady? I bet you're already in school for the day. Well I'm at work, in training. BORING. I hope you had nutrition for breakfast and not just junk food. I wanted to talk to you about what happened the other day. Look baby girl, I am so sorry! First and foremost, grades don't define your determination. You don't have bad grades because you are dumb or incapable. School sucks- I know.. People are weird, family is weird and you are navigating with little support. It's O.K. to need help! It's O.K. to need motivation and support. You are a growing young lady. You don't have to know all the answers. That 'D' means so little in the bigger picture of what makes you - YOU. You didn't deserve to be beaten like that. All because he didn't 'beat clothing'. You didn't deserve to be violated in that way. You deserved to be loved and nurtured, and to be spoken to with the softest of voices and the tightest of hugs. Not beat for getting a D in a subject that he never offered you help in. You should have been understood, heard, loved and protected. You are worth so much more than what you were given. You deserved the love that you gave so effortlessly. I know that you spend your time in your head trying to keep peace or make sense of the chaos, just keep trying! You are loved and protected beyond this realm. Keep your beautiful smile and your loving nature. You may not be able to see the light that guides you, but it is there! Never be ashamed of you! I love you more than you will ever know. I want what is absolutely best for you, and believe me you do too! I wish I could hug away your fears and kiss awayyour tears,

Love, Trisheena

Self

Your eyes did not see
Not that I cared anyway
Black been beautiful

Smooth as a cool spring Sweet as a fresh juicy peach Dark skin feeds my soul

I used to need you
I've looked away from your stare
I validate me

Fulfilled

I always wondered what it would be like to be a smile for someone. To come from within the shadows too afraid to let enough light in that I might disappear. I rested there. A strange position to be. Shining, yet feeling so dark. I often wondered what it would feel like to be laughter for someone. To be their sparkle that sits in their eye. 1016 0402 0725 1231.

Four smiles. Four billows of laughter. The joy is unmatched, but doesn't fill the void.

My love grows from me effortlessly, but my roots quenched their thirst themselves. Effortlessly. My love took a tiny seed and grew the ingredients to make a meal. Yet, no one to get the big piece of chicken. I created an environment soft enough to cradle my vulnerabilities, yet strong enough to assure them. Learning to love the life that I lived freed me. I got ready. I I started to ask myself questions. I became the partner that I wanted to be. I treated myself kinder, softer. I made peace with my trials. I took myself on dates. And adventures. I shifted toward was brightened my light. I manifested an authentic soul in partnership who could relate every situation to a song lyric. I prayed for a partner who saw light in me. Who shined light on me. My soul mate. In human form. I'm ready.

mybodyisatemple

She told me a story about a man who used to come and pick me up. He was so nice and loved me so much. He had two daughters. We would play together. Then one day he went to jail for raping and murdering his two daughters and storing them in the freezer.

Me: Do you think he ever touched me?

Her Chuckling: oh, I don't know.

Never to be discussed again...

I had to be 4. I remember there was a porno playing. We were laying on the floor. He was 7. He was humping me with my clothes off. I can remember the video, and looking at the penis and thinking the testicles were on the opposite end. He tried to insert his penis into my vagina, but it didn't go in. I felt it against my skin. Someone came in the room and grabbed him, but they left me on the floor with the movie still playing. They didn't check on me. Ever.

First time, one guy, two fingers. I was just a little girl sitting by the edge of the pool. I used to have a green and pink sparkling bathing suit with fringes. A man, I don't know who he was–I never even saw his face. This man came and picked me up from the side of the pool, walked with me into the deep waters…. Opened my legs around his waist and stuck his fingers into my vagina. Second time, the same thing happened. The second time this happened at the pool, it was a guy whose name i remember because i heard someone say it, but I don't remember his face. He did the same thing. I wasn't certain if that was the thing to do at the pool, but I went less, barely at all. I can't remember how that made me feel, But I remember it happening. I remember driving past the pool as an adult and pulling over. I prayed for that little girl, too numb to understand what was happening. I cried for her. I begged for her forgiveness....

I don't even know. His name was Michael. He was from England. His accent was so intriguing. One time he gave me $20 to sit on his lap. I told my mom. She went to the school and cursed him out and gave him the $20 back.

They grabbed me, each grabbed either my arm or a leg. They held me midair while they each took turns inserting their fingers in my vagina. I struggled. My leg fells. They ran. They are lucky because I was looking for dicks to kick.

By the time I was teen I saw more penises than I needed to... on church steps, at the bus tops, on the way to camp, on the way to the park, on the way anywhere. Disgusting men rubbing their dicks with their pants at their ankles for a little child to see them.

I had a girl fight and abuse me regularly if I didn't engage in a sexual relationship with her- I can remember it like it was yesterday. Her fingers gripped through my freshly straightened Afro and forced my face into her lap. I can still remember the smell. We were 9 years old. And I saw her getting out of a vehicle with her mother and her tricks plenty of times. Who is there to blame?

When I was 12, I really struggled. I asked for help. I sought tutoring. I simply couldn't get it together. I got a D on my report card. He never even offered to tutor me. Not sit with me when I did my homework. Not anything. He came to my house that day and learned I got a D. He tells me that the doesn't beat clothes. I say But I'm on my cycle. He doesn't care. My spirit cracked in two pieces. He lost me that day...

WHO IS THERE TO BLAME? WHO WAS SUPPOSED TO PROTECT ME? WHO IS GOING TO LIFT THE GUILT AND SHAME?

My body is a temple and its filled with love and grace.

And its mine!!!

I Am Here!

I am here!

She's here!

I am here!

Now this is what I've been waiting for

I'm here!

And it feels so good to be here.

I am here! Yessssssss I'm here.

I am HERE BABY!! ME!!!!

I am I am here I am not going anywhere because I am here.

I am Big. I am Bold. I am Beautiful

I am right here!) Yes I am honey. I am here!!!

I am here to stay with my BIG BOLD AND BEAUTIFULLY BLACK SELF.

I am here. Yes! I am here. I am here ooooooh I am here. I am here.

Self-Validation...

"I tried my best" saves the day when I feel that more could have been done.

"I tried my best" implies that there is a bar, and I came close enough.

I'm not saving anymore days from the inadequacies of I tried my best. I did an awesome job is quite sufficient.

It was Angels Who Guided Me Home.

One night I wanted to go to a party with a friend. This friend was my ace boon at one point. The party was far away, in some part of Philly that I had never even heard of. I wasn't a party type of person, but I did love to go out. So, I went to this bowling party with my friend. I didn't even have to get permission. I just told my mom I was going. I was 14. My friend had a ride for us there. We had fun, I guess. Then when it was time to go- my home girl told me that she had a ride for us with some guys. I wasn't the type of kid who really hung out with anyone let alone older guys. I was nervous but agreed because I didn't even think about a ride home before I made this plan. We got too Broad and Tioga. My friend said they weren't going to drive us all the way home and that we could go inside his house. Now I know that girl code says you never leave your friend behind. I asked her to come with me and she sided with the guys. I said LET ME OUT RIGHT HERE. It was like 2 in the morning. I was all alone. I felt betrayed. My friend would let me walk home alone instead of walking with me. She left me over some boys.

I didn't have a dad I could call to rescue me. I had no one I didn't really know my way home, but I did know how to follow street numbers. I looked for all the things I have ever noticed from taking the bus route in this neighborhood. McDonald's? Ok, make a right. Rhodes school? Yup, keep walking this way. I thought about the time I met Kwame Touré at Rhodes School when I was about 9. I remember my mom making a big deal about how far we had to walk but she was determined to get us there. He told me that I had the prettiest eyes. He was so tall and handsome. I had no idea how much of an impact his intellectual and literary contributions would be to the world and to myself. I got to Lehigh Avenue and knew my way from there. I had to come all the way to 22nd and Lehigh on numerous occasions to use the laundry mat because they had vans that would transport for a few dollars. I walked up to 29th street. I was very familiar with this neighborhood as I walked through it many times. I walked past the doctor's office that I usually went to with a note that I could get my shots alone. There was the ice-cream shop that my dad took me to as a reward for beating him in Crazy 8's. It was my first time playing and I beat him. I still love Black cherry ice cream to this day. I walked past the house where a massacre occurred. I walked past where a man held people hostage. I walked past so many empty lots that I lost count. Every corner was a trap house. I kept my head down. I sang songs to myself. I had no one to call, and no one came looking for me either. It was the Angels who guided me home.

Those eyes...

I think about you often. I don't remember what you were wearing. I pray for you. I hope that if you were given the chance, you would forgive me. When I walked past the van, I looked at him. He looked at me. He pointed to his toys. He had clackers in his van, but it was dark in there. I got to the other side of the street. I looked back. I looked at you. You looked at me. I looked away. I looked back and saw the doors close behind you. I turned around and kept walking. I think about you often. Why didn't I say something? Why didn't I yell? Why didn't I call the police? I've apologized to you so many times in my head. I've imagined you got free. Your eyes though. I promise to never be her again. I promise to always think love with your name. I promise to never let another girl... Please just set me free.

Just Breath

The candles are crackling and popping. I am in my element. I just want to sit here and take a deep breath....The music is so soft yet I feel it so loudly...Pen is in my hand but the words are staying right where they are. Barriers being broken, crumbled, close your eyes and breath.

Inhale...Exhale... just be.

Breath...I am not tryna process who I'm not, I'm blessed for who I am in this very moment. Everything changes eventually but right...I'm sitting with me.

Inhale.... I'm in my element.

Purple Flowers

I used to fear getting into trouble for telling my mother's business. I must have been five and I remember getting yelled at. I told my kindergarten teacher something about my mother that she didn't like. Something that she didn't want anyone to know about. Hide. I learned that from her that day. Hide who you are from those who may bring you shame. Still unlearning this lesson today. I have a story to tell. It's hard to get it out through the tears and uncertainty and this tremendous guilt, but the little girl inside of me has a story to tell. I...we... have a story to tell.

See don't get too sad this story is a beautiful tale that watches a girl, emotionally detached from her mother, learn love how life offers it. I came into this world with my mom unavailable. Here but not at the same time. Too occupied by her own weeds to share her flowers with me. This story is about the only person that I have ever wanted to be close to but couldn't get within enough reach.

I saw a little girl today, she did not care to speak. Strength welled in her mind, but her will was weak.

I spoke with the little girl today her eyes began to glisten. All this time no one knew she could speak, and she really just needed someone to listen.

There's a special bond that exists between a girl and her mother. Mothers are supposed to be the first ones to love you right? They are the epitome of love. Of Warmth. Of Hugs. Of Delicious foods that sit in your belly just long enough to make you smile. I spent 13 years from age 4 to 17 in one house. Flashbacks of my darkness often start in that house. Flashbacks to my mom calling me ugly and laughing at my tears I can still feel the shame that started in the house. One day when I was about 8 years old, the oil heater that house broke. Black smoke poured into the bedrooms from the basement. I was home alone due to being sick. I suffered smoke inhalation and needed to go to the Emergency Room. The Doctor there advised my mom to quit smoking around me because I would likely develop a chronic lung condition. We never even had heat in that house after that day. We used to scrape the snowflakes from the windows. I questioned love then. I took myself to the doctors when they prescribed me an inhaler for asthma. I questioned love then. I asked her over and over again to get my inhaler from the pharmacy and she wouldn't. Was that love? Or the fact that my mother didn't quit smoking until I moved out of her house? No amount of parenting myself made her love me. Why didn't I deserve her love? To this day I still don't know what she is exactly.

She wasn't loving. Or nurturing. She was always mad. Always yelling. Always cussing. Always fussing. But mostly she wasn't present. She was empty. She left feeling me emptier. I can't even really say that love lived there, nor can I say love was never present. I learned that love was a tool useful in survival, and no matter how much of her blood dripped on me, she was still just surviving. I remember my mother only ever telling me that she loved me one time. I was 11 years old. I was staying overnight with one of her friends while she was away. Before we hung up the phone, I told her that I loved her. It seemed like a normal thing to do, right? Something I had been wanting to do and being around loving strangers gave me the courage to do so. Can you imagine? Being afraid to tell your mother that you loved her. She responded, "I love you too". I still wonder if she said it by mistake that day, as she never said it again. Her response to I love you, became "yeah yeah yeah." Like she didn't even believe in it herself. My mother's love or lack of it always had me feeling alone. Always made me feel like being loved was wayyyy to much to ask for. Like love was some mythical concept too far out of reach. Sometimes I go back and forth on if I can really blame my mom though. I often wonder what type of life she lived that made her the way that she was. Like maybe her mother didn't know how to love her. And then in turn she didn't know how to love me. Deciphering my mother's behaviors and making excuses for her decisions became a skill for me. The most psychologically tortuous game that I never wanted to play. I was a child carrying the heaviness of a responsibility that I wasn't prepared for. I was a mother of three long before I birthed anyone. Trying to keep her happy with me ate me from the inside out. The ambiguity in never feeling right enough or wrong enough created a level of projected perfectionism that was truly exhausting. The only thing my mother ever seemed pleased with, was my ability to do the things that she didn't want to do. I learned to need nothing.

You see my mother likely had "issues." I can't say for certain as I am not a doctor, but I learned to make space for her invisible "issues" long before I even had the mental capacity to understand what "having issues" meant. I felt sorry for her often. Never reserving that protection for myself. Having a mom like I did. I was always left confused. Always left to figure things out on my own. Always left to navigate the ills of the world through the lens of my own limited understanding. I learned to be alone. The solitude that was once a thorn in my side became a resting place for butterflies because I no longer needed it to protect me, solitude became my closest friend. One thing that I was never confused about was wanting love. Wanting to be loved. And wanting to be heard.

I loved the little girl today.

Her heart began to smile. She became the goddess that she was meant to be, She was *fierce* and she was proud. I danced with the little girl today. I became her wildest dream. To see the *fire* in her eyes.

To see her set me free.

I needed it. Invincible, unspoken yet reciprocated love. I craved it. I sought. I worked hard for it. I attached myself to what felt like home. Looking for love within everything that I touched. When my mother told me that I was ugly like Celie [1] I marched myself down to the Free library of Philadelphia located at 19th and Vine. I took the 32 bus and got off at my stop. I searched and searched until I found it. Yes, the big 304 paged book by one of my favorite authors- Alice Walker.[2] It was too big for my bag, so I carried it. I was 8 or 9 years old. Mrs. Walker said, "I think it pisses God off if you walk past the color purple in a field and don't notice it." Reading that in a book encouraged me to ALWAYS see the purple flowers. There's love in those flowers. There always has been. There was love in the desire to read the book of every movie that I felt a connection with. There was love in pretzel day, and Girl scout troop 83, and the corner store owner – Mr. Sam?! Mr. Sam had the flyest shiniest roundest Afro I've ever seen. He always let me go when I didn't have enough money. One time I stole a 10 cents pack of sunflower seeds from the counter of his store. I felt guilty and brought them back. I wrote him a letter apologizing. Mr. Sam bought me a word processor so that I could be successful in school. He saw so much promise in me even after I stole those Sunflower seeds. Maybe that's why I love sunflowers so much. There was love in the clothespin at 15th and market that took my breath away every time I looked at the top from the very bottom.

---

1 Celie, The Color Purple, Steven Spielberg 1985
2 The Color Purple, Alice Walker 1982

My mom would take me downtown with her when she had to pay her credit card bills. There was love in my fourth-grade teacher Mrs. Walker catching me in the coat closet with a boy. But allowing me to continue to meet him there because he got letters from his dad in jail and couldn't read them himself. There Is love in homemade pancakes with no recipe and trips to the farm for fresh eggs and picking the juiciest strawberries there and eating them without even rinsing them off. There was love in my cousin Tanisha teaching me all about the unique delicateness of snowflakes and then catching them on my tongue. There was love in teaching myself how to meditate when I had trouble connecting to God. There was even love in my mother failing to see beauty in my face because it led me to seeing the purple flowers I found love all around me. And now I live it every single day.

Flowers into the ears of my babies that I am blessed to have and nurture, I exhale those three words like breath from my lungs. I LOVE YOU. There's love in the gardens that I tend to, that I feed and that I feed my babies from. Their lives are the manifestation of my hearts wildest desire. of beautiful fruits harvested from a tree with damaged roots. Of the love that life so bountifully offers when you must seek it. I have found love. And now, instead of living instability, uncertainty, and indifference, I am living, breathing and being love.

I uncaged that little girl today. I unclipped her wings. To watch her dance across the sky, now she is free just to be
L-O-V-E.

Love

Please look in my eyes

You will see serenity Or

look at my smile

Fierceness is a trait Or

just an acquired taste

Either way I'm fierce

I'm not anti you

But I am in love with me

You should love me too

Serving You My Flowers

Life gives nothing, you receive what you take from it. Reciprocate good energy, don't cheat and don't quit. No one in this world can take you away from you. Love you, forgive you. Always be your best you, for you. Your powers manifest from the inside out. Speak love to yourself, and love the truth that comes out. Shake some tables, the proverbial kind. There is power in your choices be smart but be kind. Don't dumb yourself down be big in every space if you need to delegate be smart don't wait. I love you, and Ill always be around. Thruough every win, bad choice, I'm at the front of crowd. Love is a journey not a place to take a trip. Just don't forget even flowers can smell like shit.

I've Let Them Go Y'all...

Burning sage

Eyes closed, breathing slowed

Guided meditations on repeat.

I've cried...

I've let them go y'all.

I still hear my name being called when I wake up. My name Yelled with the scent of disdain, dissatisfactions. What did I do now? I still feel the inadequacies of projected perfection. Disappointment every time she looked at me. I have to blink my eyes to control the impact of the flash back.

I've let them go y'all

They say family are your first true friends. Maybe that's why I never understood friendship. Maybe that's why I would get that uncomfortable feeling from my spine up to my eyebrows whenever someone considered me.

I've let them go y'all

I used to get up and relock locked doors. Flashbacks of getting beat while looking at the teenage shame of a bloody pad in the seat of my panties on the floor. All for getting a d in a subject that no one offered to tutor me in. My dad had a baby that at year. I spent more time with him- because he needed a baby-sitter. I loved that little girl.

Did I let them go y'all?

I had to tell myself that placing an obligation to sacrifice will not also force someone to show you appreciation. You cannot force reciprocity. Reciprocal energy needs to exist in a space where my heart has no guards. I cannot hide from my vulnerabilities.

I've done it. I've let them go y'all!!

Crying in the middle of the bathroom floor why don't they love me?

Mind blanked at the red lights, cars honking ... But do they have to hate me?

Smiling at myself in the mirror -Why is my happiness- a bad thing?

But I've let them go...y'all.

When I'm alone at times they own my thoughts. Calculating all the energy I have given to people who are consistently subtracting the blessings... Looking to me to fix it, who is going to fix me?

I need to let them go y'all.

Fighting my self-worth, I've driven thousands of miles to see smiles on faces that have ridiculed and made a mockery of mine. Just to break bread with the broken.

I've got to let them go YALL.   Can I let them go y'all?

What about family togetherness? No more over-priced and underwhelming family vacations that separated us more than they could ever bring us together.

I can let them go y'all.

This peace...mmmmhhhmmm this peace tastes like chicken and dumplings. This peace feels like a blanket fresh out of the dryer. This peace...mmmhmmmm this peace. Nurturing that baby that they failed to love. Loving on the little girl they failed to nourish and saluting the woman that they failed to prepare.

Finally, I have let them go.... Y'all

Deep Breath

So what did you think? I know, some if this was heavy. Take a deep breath and let some of that energy go. I know some if it took you to a place or time that wasn't the healthiest for you. But guess what? Healing is the key and the goal. Close your eyes and breath in.

If you or anyone that you know is being hurt, abused or neglected, please speak up!

Help is available

National Domestic Violence Hotline
Hours: 24/7   800-799-7233

Report Child Abuse

1-800-422-4453

It can be intimidating to report child abuse, but reporting it yourself has significant advantages. Providing firsthand details gives child-care workers more accurate information than hearing it secondhand. Do not allow fear to prevent you from reporting; Empower yourself to speak up and advocate for yourself. You've got this!

It took me a long time to learn self value. Report your abuse now... For the you who will lay awake wishing that you did.

Don't Get Too Used To Just Enough.

Because you won't have anywhere to put all of your bigger stuff, you learn really quick you also got to be just tough just enough.

Just enough fills the room

Just enough never moves

Just enough hovers happiness just to disapprove.

This room fits just enough oh so well.

Just enough gets big but just enough doesn't swell

You get just enough happy, just enough smiles; just enough laughter to last a little while.

Just enough fuel to create a small spark. But you carry way too much *light*, it outshines just enough dark.

Just enough breaks hearts. Just enough can't feel. Just enough steals joy. Just enough can't heal.

Don't be afraid to be large, bold and bright.

Bring peace, bring joy bring *all of your light*.

Take up this space above and beyond but this time- just for you, because just enough once lied, you are more than enough for this room.

Light Incoming

The sun shines so bright when the darkness fades.

Let the sunshine in welcome the beams and the rays.

Watch it reflect off the things - leaving the shadow just behind

Let the sunshine in face the world you will be fine.

The sun shines so bright when you open the blinds-

So do, it right now..

Be quick but take Your time.

Let the sun melt your fingers flex your pointer and your thumb.

I know it might seem silly stretch your face, stick out your tongue.
Bend your toes, shake out your legs. Interpret that how you may.
The sun is going to shine how it shines anyway.

I will not defend me
My beauty needs no defense
It is and will be

SELF LOVE JOURNEY IN HAIKU

www.ingramcontent.com/pod-product-compliance
Lightning Source LLC
Chambersburg PA
CBHW030226170426
43194CB00007BA/881